SIKH
Prayer and Worship

Rajinder Singh Panesar/Anita Ganeri

W
FRANKLIN WATTS
LONDON • SYDNEY

First published in 2006 by
Franklin Watts
338 Euston Road
London NW1 3BH

Franklin Watts Australia
Hachette Children's Books
Level 17/207 Kent Street
Sydney NSW2000

Editor: Rachel Cooke
Design: Joelle Wheelwright
Picture research: Diana Morris
Acknowledgements:
Chris Fairclough/Franklin Watts: 8, 18, 21. Hutchison/Eye Ubiquitous: front cover b, 29.
Jenny Matthews/Franklin Watts: 6, 19. Richard T. Nowitz/Corbis: 5.
Christine Osborne/World Religions Photo Library: front cover c, 26. Rajinder Singh
Panesar: 9, 11, 12, 14, 15, 16, 20. Helene Rogers/Ark Religion: 10, 13, 22, 25, 27.
Steve Shott/Franklin Watts: 7, 17, 23, 28. Liba Taylor/Hutchison/Eye Ubiquitous: 24.
Every attempt has been made to clear copyright. Should there be any inadvertent
omission please apply to the publisher for rectification.

A CIP catalogue record for this book is available
from the British Library.
Dewey Decimal Classification Number: 294.6

ISBN-10: 0 7496 5939 4
ISBN-13: 978 0 7496 5939 4

Printed in China

This Sikh symbol is called the Khanda.
The double-edged sword at its centre
represents the one creative power of God
above the universe.

Contents

The prayers in this book were chosen by Rajinder Singh Panesar. Rajinder is a practising Sikh who works for the Bradford Interfaith Education Centre as a Sikh faith tutor. Rajinder also teaches Sikhism and Punjabi language in schools, colleges and gurdwaras. He is involved in many gurdwaras and other Sikh organisations both locally, in West Yorkshire, and nationally, around the UK.

About Sikhism

Sikhs are followers of a religion called Sikhism which began about 500 years ago in the Punjab region of northwest India. At that time, the main religions in India were Hinduism and Islam but there were many conflicts between the two. A holy man, called Nanak (1469-1539), introduced a new religion which taught equality and tolerance. He became the first of the ten Sikh Gurus, or holy teachers.

This is the symbol of Ik Onkar, which means 'one God'.

Sikh beliefs

Sikhs believe in Ik Onkar which means 'one God'. They believe that God exists in everyone and everything in the universe, and that, therefore, everyone and everything is equal. Sikhs hope to grow closer to God by remembering God in everything they do. This makes praying to and praising God an essential part of a Sikh's life.

There is only one God and God is the only truth. God the creator is without fear, without hate and immortal. God is beyond death and is understood through God's grace.

About this prayer

This is the first verse of the Mool Mantar which means 'basic teaching'. The prayer forms the first paragraph of the Guru Granth Sahib, the Sikhs' holy book (see page 7). It sums up what Sikhs believe about God. God cannot be seen but is always present and everywhere. God was not born and will not die.

Three golden rules

Sikhs also follow three golden rules which were given to them by Guru Nanak. These are:

1) Nam japna: Meditating on God's name. Praying to and thinking about God is very important. Guru Nanak said that when people pray to God, it is the only time that their minds have a chance to rest.

2) Kirat karna: Earning an honest living. Working hard is part of being a Sikh. Guru Nanak said that if Sikhs feed their families with money earned in a dishonest way, their children may grow up to be bad people.

3) Vand chhakna: Sharing our time and earnings with needy people. Guru Nanak instructed Sikhs to share 10 per cent of their earnings with needy people and to spend 10 per cent of their time working for good causes.

Sikhs around the world

Today there are about 14 million Sikhs. Most still live in India but through emigration, strong Sikh communities have grown up in the UK, Canada, Australia and the USA.

A Sikh place of worship is called a gurdwara. This beautiful one is in Canada.

Sikh Prayer and Worship

For Sikhs, saying prayers is a way of spending time in God's company. Even though they cannot see God, they feel able to pray to God as a caring friend. Some Sikhs like to visit a gurdwara, the Sikh place of worship, to pray in the presence of the Guru Granth Sahib, the holy book. Most Sikhs also worship at home.

Sikh prayers

There are two kinds of Sikh prayers. The first kind is set prayers which Sikhs say every day at home or in the gurdwara, in the morning, evening and before going to sleep. These prayers are called Nit nem (see page 10). The second kind is personal prayers which Sikhs can say anywhere and at any time. Sikh prayers may be read or sung as songs. They are said in the Punjabi language and written down in Gurmukhi script.

A boy says his evening prayers before going to sleep. When Sikhs pray they usually close their eyes and put the palms of their hands together.

The Guru Granth Sahib

Most Sikh prayers come from the Guru Granth Sahib, the holy book of the Sikhs. When the tenth Sikh Guru, Gobind Singh (1666-1708) was dying, he did not name a person to succeed him as Guru. Instead, he said that the Guru Granth Sahib should be the Sikh's everlasting guide. The Guru Granth Sahib is a collection of hymns and verses, written by Guru Nanak and five of the other Gurus, together with Hindu and Muslim holy men. Prayers also come from the Dasam Granth, a collection of hymns by Guru Gobind Singh, and from the songs of a Sikh scholar called Bhai Gurdas (c.1551-1637).

Sikhs treat the Guru Granth Sahib with great respect as they believe it contains the word of God, passed on by the Gurus.

Blessed is the hour when I see You.
I am glad to be in Your presence.
You are the giver of my life,
my beloved God;
I maintain my whole being by
keeping You in mind.
Your teaching is true,
Your word is sweet,
Your eyes see everything,
You are calmness itself.
Your patience is the
source of my peace,
Your law is unchanging, my Lord.
My God is beyond birth and death.

About this prayer
This is a prayer from the Guru Granth Sahib which is recited when a copy of the Guru Granth Sahib is installed in a gurdwara or in a Sikh's home. It was written by the fifth Sikh Guru, Arjan (1536-1606). After the prayer is said, everyone bows and sits down. A granthi (see page 9) then reads from the Guru Granth Sahib. For some Sikhs, it is as though their Guru is whispering words of wisdom in their ears.

Worship in the Gurdwara

A gurdwara is a place where Sikhs meet to worship. The word 'gurdwara' means 'the door of the Guru'. Any place where the Guru Granth Sahib has been installed can be a gurdwara. However, worshipping together is important for Sikhs because it shows that everyone is equal and part of one family. So if possible, Sikhs visit the gurdwara twice a day to say their prayers in the presence of the Guru Granth Sahib. But many Sikhs only visit at the weekend or on special occasions or festivals. Sikh children worship in the gurdwara with their parents and quickly learn the words of the prayers.

Before entering the prayer hall, Sikhs take off their shoes and cover their heads. The worshippers face the Guru Granth Sahib which is on a raised platform or throne, under a canopy.

Worship in the gurdwara

There is no special day for worship in the gurdwara but the main service is held on a Sunday to fit in with the working week. Each gurdwara has a granthi who leads the prayers in Punjabi. The granthi is a devout Sikh and may be a man or a woman. Services include kirtan (hymn singing), prayers and talks about Sikh history. A prayer called the Ardas is said at the end of the service. Afterwards, the granthi opens the Guru Granth Sahib at random and reads out a verse of guidance for the day.

At the end of the service special food, called karah prasad, is shared out among worshippers.

*True are Your worlds,
true are Your universes.
True are Your realms,
true is Your creation.
True are Your actions,
and all Your deliberations.
True is Your command,
and true is Your justice.
True is Your will,
true is Your order.
True is Your mercy,
true is Your authority.
Hundreds of thousands and
millions call You true.
In the true Lord is all power, in
the true Lord is all might.
True is Your praise,
true is Your adoration.
True is all that You have created.
O Nanak, true are those who
meditate on the True One.*

About this prayer

This is most of one verse (there are 83 in total) from a prayer called the Asa di Var written by Guru Nanak. It talks about the authority of God and praises God and true religion. God is the only truth and everything about God is true. Sikhs believe that people who meditate on and pray to God are true devotees of God. This prayer is sung to open the morning service in the gurdwara.

Daily Prayers

The first golden rule or teaching of Guru Nanak is meditating on God's name (see page 5). This means praying to God and thanking God for everything God has provided us with. By saying set daily prayers, in the morning, evening and at bedtime, Sikhs seek to follow this teaching. These prayers are called Nit nem meaning 'daily routine'.

These worshippers have found a quiet place for morning prayers facing the Golden Temple, Amritsar, Punjab.

O Lord God,
You are without any form,
class or symbol.
None can describe Your form,
features or shape.
Eternal and unchanging,
Shining brightly in
Your own light,
Your power is without any limit.
You are the Lord of Lords,
King of Kings.
Master of the three worlds,
You rule over gods,
men and demons.
Even the blades of grass
in the forest,
Proclaim Your infinity.
Who can ever recite all
your names!
By Your deeds alone can
You be known.

About this prayer

This is a verse from another morning prayer called the Jap Sahib. It comes from the Dasam Granth which was composed by Guru Gobind Singh. The prayer is 199 verses long and describes and praises God. Sikhs believe that praising God brings happiness, prosperity and peace of mind.

Morning prayers

Sikhs try to get up early in the morning, around four or five o'clock. This time is known as amrit vela which means 'the holy time before dawn'. After a bath, Sikhs find a quiet place where they can sit to say their five set morning prayers. Some Sikhs know these prayers by heart while others use a gutka (prayer book). Once these prayers have been said, Sikhs stand and offer their personal prayers to God.

Air is the Guru, Water is the
Father, and Earth is the
Great Mother of all.
Day and night are the
guardians, caring
for all creation.
In the Court of the Lord, the
record of good and bad
deeds is read out.
According to our own
actions, we are drawn
closer, or are driven
further away.
Those who have faithfully
meditated on the
Name of the Lord,
Their work is done. They are
free and others with them.
O Nanak, radiantly
they go to glory!

Guru Nanak wrote many prayers, including the Japji Sahib.

About this prayer

This prayer is the last verse of the Japji Sahib, one of the set morning prayers. It was composed by Guru Nanak and is found at the beginning of the Guru Granth Sahib. Through this prayer, Sikhs praise God and understand the importance of praying to God. The prayer tells how the souls of those who have led a good life will, one day, become one with God (see pages 24-25 for more about Sikh beliefs about life and death).

Evening prayers

There are no set prayers for Sikhs to say during the day, although many people say their own private prayers. After work, Sikhs wash in preparation for the Rehras Sahib, the set evening prayer. As in the morning, they choose a quiet place where they can concentrate on God. If possible, they sit cross-legged to recite the evening prayer by heart, or read it from a gutka. The prayer takes about 15 minutes. In many households, one person recites the prayer and the whole family joins in. After reciting the Rehras Sahib, Sikhs say a personal prayer asking God to forgive them for their wrong-doings.

A family says their evening prayers together. On the wall behind them is a picture of the Golden Temple at Amritsar.

Hearing of Your greatness, everyone calls You great.
Yet it is only by seeing that we know how great You are.
Your worth cannot be estimated. You cannot be described.
Those who have glimpsed it are full of Your praises.
Great is my Master, beyond comprehending,
His virtues transcendent, divine.
None may know the extent of Your might and magnificence.
None may describe Your true worth.
Scholars, holy teachers and men of devotion study the scriptures.
But even they cannot describe Your greatness.
All goodness and truth, all spiritual powers,
All of these come from You.
They cannot be achieved without Your grace and mercy.
Wonderful is Your storehouse, filled with treasure.
What need have we of help when our Master supports us,
The True One who comforts and guides.

About this prayer

The set prayer in the evening is called the Rehras Sahib. The verses above are part of it. The prayer is a collection of hymns composed by five different Gurus. Most of the prayer is found in the Guru Granth Sahib. The parts composed by Guru Gobind Singh (right) are recorded in the Dasam Granth. Through this prayer, Sikhs thank God that the day has passed in happiness. They thank God for being merciful and protecting them.

Bedtime prayers

The final set prayer of the day is called the Kirtan Sohila. It is recited at night before you go to sleep. For this reason, it is not a very long prayer because people may be tired. The purpose of the prayer is to turn your mind away from the cares and concerns of the day to focus on God.

Hymn of joy

Kirtan Sohila means 'hymn of joy'. This prayer is actually made up of five hymns. Three were composed by Guru Nanak; one by the fourth Guru, Ram Das (1534-1581), and one by Guru Arjan. Apart from at bedtime, this prayer is also recited when a person dies (see pages 24-25). Through the prayer, Sikhs ask God for the courage and strength to face discomfort and death. It is believed that those who say this prayer sincerely will not be afraid of death. It is also recited in the gurdwara when the copy of the Guru Granth Sahib is put to rest at the end of the day.

Bedtime prayers help Sikhs to leave behind the worries of the day.

14

When we are gathered to worship the Master,
Sing to His praises and ponder His name.
Sing to His glory, reflect on His wonders,
He who is Lord and Creator of all.
Sing to His praises, our Lord who is fearless.
Humbly, I bow for the song which brings joy.
He who gives life is our constant Protector,
Watching and guarding us, safe in His care.
How can we judge all His goodness and mercies,
How grasp the worth of His marvellous grace?
God has determined the time for my nuptials,
Come pour the oil of joy at my door.
Bless me, my friends, that I find this sweet union,
Dwelling as one with my Master and Lord.
All must receive their last call from the Master,
Daily He summons those souls who must go.
Hold in remembrance the Lord who will summon you.
Soon you will hear His command.

About this prayer

This is the first hymn of the Kirtan Sohila prayer. It was composed by Guru Nanak. Through this hymn, Sikhs remember God as powerful and fearless. They ask Him for protection, as their master and provider of countless blessings. Since God has decided on everyone's last day on Earth, Sikhs request their friends to pray for them and give them good wishes so that they can unite with God as in a marriage (nuptials). This union with God is something all Sikhs hope for.

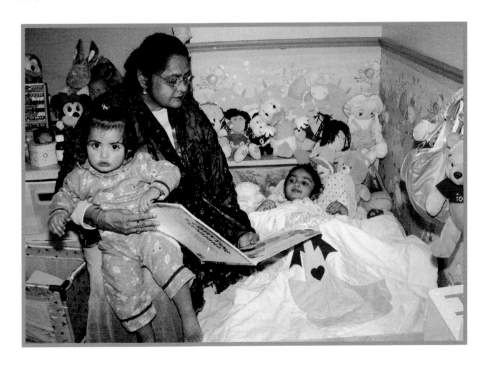

After a bedtime story, grandparents often recite the Kirtan Sohila to their grandchildren so that the children do not have nightmares.

Worship at Home

Saying the set prayers is very important for Sikhs, whether at the gurdwara or at home. Some families pray together in the morning or evening. They believe that praying together helps to strengthen family ties. Some children get up a few minutes early to recite a short, personal prayer.

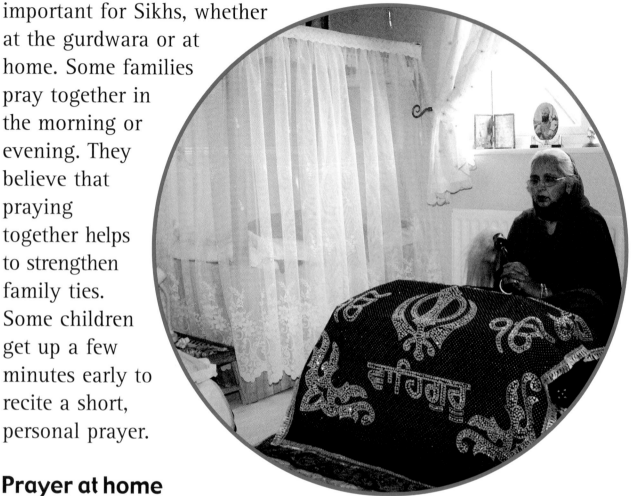

Prayer at home

Some Sikh households have a special room or corner of a room which is set aside for prayer. This is where they keep a copy of the Guru Granth Sahib. Each morning, they open the Guru Granth Sahib, then perform their daily prayers. If Sikhs do not have a copy of the Guru Granth Sahib at home, they can visit the gurdwara at any time to pray in its presence. They may also say prayers as they are walking to school or travelling to work.

The corner of this room has been set aside for the Guru Granth Sahib. It has a special curtained area where it is kept at night.

Praying for others

The Guru Granth Sahib teaches Sikhs the importance of caring for and helping other people, as a way of worshipping God. This is called sewa (service). Sewa might mean doing work in the gurdwara, or giving money to the poor. It also means finding time to pray for others. Sikhs believe that praying for others makes you humble and pleases God. The person you pray for may, in turn, pray to God for you.

Sikh children put coins in a money box inside a gurdwara as part of sewa.

You are our Lord and Master.
To You, I offer this prayer.
This body and soul belong to You.
You are our mother and father.
We are Your children.
In Your grace, there are so many joys!
No one knows Your limits.
O Highest of the High, most Generous God,
The whole of creation is strung
on Your thread.
That which has come from
You is under Your command.
You alone know Your state and extent.

About this prayer
This verse comes from a prayer called the Sukhmani Sahib which means 'hymn of peace'. It was composed by Guru Arjan and is found in the Guru Granth Sahib. This is a prayer which Sikh children like to say to seek God's peace and blessing. Some children know the words by heart or read them from a gutka. Others will sit quietly and repeat the word 'Waheguru'. This is the Sikh name for God.

Prayers over Meals

Sikhs believe that God created the world and everything in it. Among God's creations is the food we eat every day. Sikhs accept food as a gift from God which must be respected. Without food, there would be no life on Earth. Before and after Sikhs eat their meals, they say prayers to thank God and to ask for God's blessings.

Desire, anger, greed and attachment,
May these be gone,
and selfishness as well.
Nanak seeks the sanctuary of God.
Please bless me with
Your grace, O divine Guru.
O Nanak, the loaves of bread are
baked and placed on the plate.
Those who obey their Guru,
eat and feel full.
O Nanak, Guru Gobind Singh,
Guru Granth Sahib,
Thank You for this food.
I thank You for Your kindness
And I seek Your permission to begin.

About this prayer

This is a prayer which a devout Sikh says before a meal. It comes from the Sukhmani Sahib (see page 17) by Guru Arjan. It asks God to remove worldly desires and for permission to start the meal. It also thanks Him for the food.

↑ *These Sikhs are sharing*
a meal called langar.

Sharing food

All Sikh gurdwaras have a dining room (langar) where people share a meal, also called langar, together at the end of a service. It is always vegetarian so that everyone can share in the food. People take turns to help prepare and serve the meal. Everyone is welcome, Sikh or non-Sikh, and it is given for free. The custom of langar dates from Guru Nanak's time. He taught that everyone should eat together to show that everyone is equal in God's eyes.

The gurdwara kitchen where langar is cooked.

The One Lord is the Great Giver.
He is the Giver to all.
There is no limit to His Giving.
His countless storehouses are overflowing

Let us all celebrate Him, from whom we receive our nourishment.
O Nanak, no one can issue commands to the Lord our Master.
Let us offer prayers instead.
Nanak says, O God may Your name excel in the world,
And may Your grace bring peace and prosperity to the whole world.

About this prayer
This prayer may be said after a meal. It was written by Guru Arjan and is found in the Guru Granth Sahib. By saying this prayer, Sikhs accept that there is only one God who provides for everyone. Sikhs believe no one can order God to give us food, but instead, Sikhs should pray to God to give them His blessing, kindness and fulfilment.

Birthday Prayers

Guru Nanak taught that Sikhs should lead a family life and this is very important to Sikhs. A baby, a new member of the family, is received as a blessing from God. It is the duty of Sikhs to show honour and respect to this newcomer.

A grandfather whispers 'Satnam Waheguru' to a new born baby.

Naming a baby

When a baby is born, the words 'Satnam Waheguru' (Truth is the name of the wonderful Lord) are whispered into its ear. A few weeks later, the parents take the baby to the gurdwara to thank God for its arrival. After the usual service, the granthi says a prayer:

'O God, by Your Grace,
this family has a gift of a child.
Please give us a letter for
the name of this child.'

Then the granthi opens the Guru Granth Sahib at random. He reads out the first word on the left-hand page. The parents use the first letter of this word to choose a name for their baby. Once the name is chosen, it must be announced to the congregation in the presence of the Guru Granth Sahib.

↑ Parents with their baby at his naming ceremony.

God has broken every barrier, pain and sorrow swept away. Blissful joy to all who know Him, all to whom He gives His grace.

Joy abounds in all creation, praise Him you who love your Lord, God Almighty, perfect Master, all pervading, everywhere. God's eternal word has reached us, chasing far our grief and care. God is gracious, filled with mercy, Nanak thus proclaims this truth.

God has sent this wondrous gift; born of grace, may his life be long. Boundless the joy of his mother's heart, when the child appeared in her womb.

Born our son, born to adore, faithful disciple of God. His fate inscribed since time began, now given for all to see.

About this prayer

This prayer is said at the naming ceremony by the granthi and a member of the child's family. Sikhs use it to thank God for a wonderful gift of a baby. They realise that life is worthless without God's blessing and grace.

Wedding Prayers

Guru Nanak taught that marriage is very precious. All of the Sikh Gurus (apart from Guru Har Krishan who died as a child) were married. A Sikh wedding may be held in the gurdwara or in the bride's home, but it must take place in the presence of the Guru Granth Sahib.

A bride's father gives one end of the pala to the bride at a Sikh wedding.

The wedding ceremony

The Sikh wedding ceremony is called Anand karaj which means 'ceremony of bliss'. During the ceremony, the bride and groom sit in front of the Guru Granth Sahib. They listen to a talk by the granthi which reminds them of the importance of marriage and of their duties to each other. Then the bride's father gives one end of the groom's pala (scarf) to the bride. This is a symbol that they are being joined together as husband and wife.

Four circles

The most important part of the ceremony is the reading of the wedding hymn which is called the Lavan. The granthi reads the first four verses, then they are sung by the ragis (musicians). As each of the verses is sung, the couple walk around the Guru Granth Sahib. After each circle, they bow to the holy book. When they have completed the fourth circle, they are married.

Musicians often accompany hymns in the gurdwara and play a particularly important role at weddings.

I am joyously married, O Father.
I have found my Lord by my Guru's grace.
Gone is the darkness of ignorance.
The Guru has shown me His great light.
The darkness flees as His light shines forth,
The light which reveals my Lord.
The sickness of selfishness is gone now,
All pride consumed by His grace.
I have found my Lord, my immortal King,
He who is free from the chains of death.
The treasure is mine, my heart
leaps with joy.
I have found my way to my
husband's home.
My sorrows have vanished and gone.

About this prayer
The Lavan was composed by Guru Ram Das for his own daughter's wedding. The word Lavan means 'circling of the scriptures'. The first four verses are sung while the couple circle the Guru Granth Sahib. This hymn is sung by the musicians at the end of the Anand karaj (wedding) when the couple declare that, by the grace of God, their marriage is now complete. The hymn talks about the joy of marriage, the devotion of the bride and groom to each other, and about their devotion to God.

Death and Final Prayers

Sikhs believe that everyone comes into this world with the time and place of their death already written. Sikhs are sad when a loved one dies but believe that this is God's will and that God will watch over them.

When a Sikh dies, there is a special reading of the Guru Granth Sahib, from beginning to end.

Life and death

Sikhs believe that, when you die, your soul is reborn in another body. This happens over and over again. The quality of your next life depends on karma (your actions and their effects). Good actions bring a higher rebirth, closer to God. Bad actions lead you further away. If people worship God with all their hearts, God will free them from the cycle, and their souls will become one with God. This is called mukti (salvation). To achieve mukti, a person must be gurmukh (filled with God).

Sikh mourners gather around a coffin to say prayers.

Funeral prayers

When a Sikh dies, people sing hymns and read from the Guru Granth Sahib to bring comfort. They begin to read the Guru Granth Sahib right through from beginning to end, completing their reading at the time of the funeral. The funeral begins with prayers, then more prayers are said as the body is cremated. Afterwards, the mourners go to the gurdwara to complete the funeral service.

Hear, my friends, the time has come to serve all those who love the Lord.
In this world, you earn the profit of God's Name. Then you shall dwell in peace.
Day and night our end draws nearer.
Seek the Guru, be prepared!
Fear and evil rule the world. Only those that know God are saved.
Only those who God has awakened come to know the truth.
Purchase only that for which you came into the world. God's grace will lead you on.
God will dwell in your heart and end this weary cycle of death and rebirth.
All-knowing God who made us, grant this dearest wish, I pray.
Grant your slave the joy of serving all who praise the Name.

About this prayer

This prayer is the last verse of the Kirtan Sohila prayer (see page 14). Sikhs chant it together to ask for God's blessing so that they can break free from the cycle of birth and death. In this way, they hope that their souls will be united with God. The Kirtan Sohila is also the Sikh bedtime prayer. Sikhs think of death as being like a long sleep. You go to sleep in one world and wake up in another.

Festival Prayers

There are two kinds of Sikh festival - *gurpurbs* and *jore melas*. 'Gurpurb' means a 'Guru's day' and these festivals remember the lives of the ten Sikh Gurus. 'Jore' means 'a gathering' and 'mela' means 'a funfair'. These festivals celebrate other events from Sikh history.

A Sikh bows before Guru Nanak's portrait. The Guru's birthday is a gurpurb.

Guru Nanak's birthday

Guru Nanak's birthday is marked in November. He was born in 1469 in northwest India (now Pakistan). When he was about 30 years old, God told him to teach people how to live good and holy lives. Nanak's birthday is celebrated with an akhand path (a continous reading of the Guru Granth Sahib), services in the gurdwara and street processions.

The merciful Lord heard the cries of humanity
And sent Guru Nanak to this earth.
He prayed to God in utter humility and gave
God's Name to his followers.
In the dreadful Dark Ages,
Guru Nanak sang God's praise.
The Guru established the Sikh religion
And brought all people together.

About this prayer

This prayer is part of a popular hymn sung on Guru Nanak's birthday. It describes how Guru Nanak established Sikhism, a religion which treats everyone equally. The hymn was written by Bhai Gurdas (see page 7), Guru Arjan's uncle. Bhai Gurdas wrote many hymns about Sikh beliefs, history and the Gurus.

Baisakhi

Baisakhi is a jore mela which Sikhs celebrate on 13 or 14 April. It marks a very important event in Sikh history - the founding of the Khalsa (Sikh community) by Guru Gobind Singh in 1699. This is a time when many young Sikhs formally join the Khalsa at a special ceremony held in the gurdwara. They drink amrit (holy water) and promise to follow the Gurus' teachings.

These Sikhs flag bearers are dressed in traditional clothes (bana) to lead a Baisakhi parade.

O God grant me this wish that I may never refrain from doing good deeds. May I fight without any fear in life's battles, With confident courage may I claim the victory, May Your glory be fixed in my mind. May my highest ambition be singing Your praises. When this mortal life reaches its limits, May I die with limitless courage.

About this prayer
At Baisakhi, Sikhs recite this prayer which was composed by Guru Gobind Singh. Many Sikhs consider this to be their special anthem. The prayers ask for God's blessing to make Sikhs strong, humble but, at the same time, fearless in fighting for their faith.

Prayers for Peace

In their history, the Sikhs have fought many battles for their faith and to defend the rights of the weak and poor. They earned a reputation for their military strength. But Sikhs are peace-loving people. Twice, every day, they say prayers for the peace and prosperity of the world and for people everywhere.

Peace for the world

Sikhs believe that it is wrong to treat people differently or with a lack of care and consideration. After all, they are fellow human beings and live on the same Earth. Sikhs believe that everyone is equal and that everyone should be shown respect. Therefore, the prayer for peace (above right) has become an essential part of Sikh daily worship.

The world is going up in flames, Shower it with Your Mercy, and save it! Save it, and deliver it, by whatever method it takes. The True Guru has shown the way to peace, Meditating on God's Name. Nanak knows no other than the Lord God, who is the Forgiving Lord.

About this prayer

This prayer was written by the Guru Amar Das and is found in the Guru Granth Sahib. Sikhs normally try to say this prayer twice a day. Through the prayer, they ask God for mercy and peace on Earth, and for the protection of all human beings.

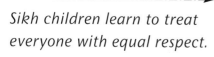

Sikh children learn to treat everyone with equal respect.

Peace of mind

Sikhs also say prayers for their own peace of mind. They believe that you should be at peace with yourself before you can give anyone else peace of mind. It is essential to be peaceful before preaching to other people about peace.

This Sikh man is sitting peacefully as he reads his prayers.

Eternal peace and bliss have come,
I have known God, who is so pleasing to my mind.
The Perfect Guru showered me with His mercy, and set me free.
My mind is filled with loving worship of the Lord.
The Lord is my all-powerful shelter and support,
I no longer depend on other people.
In great joy, I sing the glorious praises of the Lord.

About this prayer
This prayer was composed by Guru Arjan and comes from the Guru Granth Sahib. It reminds Sikhs that, by praying to God, they can achieve peace in this world and forever. By singing the praise of God the mind becomes happy and joyful. God provides support, wisdom and shelter. With this in mind, a Sikh is encouraged to help and support others to be at peace.

Glossary

Amrit vela The hour before dawn which is especially precious for prayer.

Anand karaj The Sikh wedding ceremony which takes place in front of the Guru Granth Sahib. The words 'Anand karaj' mean 'ceremony of bliss'.

Ardas The formal Sikh prayer said at the end of services in the gurdwara and on other religious occasions.

Cremated Burnt to ashes.

Dasam Granth A collection of hymns by Guru Gobind Singh, collected together some years after his death.

Emigration When people leave one country to live and work in another.

Golden Temple The gurdwara in Amritsar, India, built by Guru Arjan, and the most important building in Sikhism. It is also called the Harimandir which means 'temple of God'.

Granthi The Sikh who reads from the Guru Granth Sahib and conducts ceremonies in the gurdwara.

Gurdwara The Sikh place of worship which contains a copy of the Guru Granth Sahib. The word 'gurdwara' means 'the door to the Guru'.

Gurmukhi The script in which the Punjabi language and the Sikh scriptures are written. 'Gurmukh' means 'from the Guru's mouth'.

Gutka The Sikh prayer book which contains the words of the daily Nit nem prayers.

Guru Granth Sahib The collection of Sikh scriptures compiled by Guru Arjan and given its final form by Guru Gobind Singh. It is also called the Adi Granth which means 'first book'.

Gurus The ten great Sikh teachers who lived between 1469 and 1708. They practised Sikh teachings and led the developing Sikh community.

Ik Onkar 'Ik Onkar' means 'there is only one God', a key Sikh belief. Ik Onkar is often shown as a symbol.

Karah prasad A sweet food made from flour, sugar and butter which is shared out at the end of Sikh gatherings to symbolise equality.

Karma The belief that every action, good or bad, has a consequence which affects how a person will be reborn. Good actions bring a higher rebirth; bad actions a lower one.

Kirtan Singing the hymns and prayers found in the Guru Granth Sahib.

Khalsa The community of true and devout Sikhs.

Langar The word 'langar' means 'Guru's kitchen'. It is used to describe the dining room in the gurdwara and the food that is served in it.

Mool Mantar The prayer which forms the opening of the Guru Granth Sahib. The words 'Mool Mantar' mean 'basic teaching' and the prayer is a basic statement of Sikh belief.

Nit nem Set prayers which Sikhs say every day, in the morning, evening and before going to sleep.

Punjabi The language of the Punjab region of northwest India where Sikhism began. Sikh prayers are said in Punjabi.

Ragis These are Sikh musicians who play during the singing of hymns and prayers.

Sewa A word meaning 'service', an essential part of Sikh life and beliefs. Sewa is directed at other Sikhs, the gurdwara and people in general.

Further information

Books to read
Sacred Texts: the Guru Granth Sahib
Anita Ganeri, Evans Brothers 2003

Sikh Festivals Through the Year
Anita Ganeri, Franklin Watts 2003

Religion in Focus: Sikhism
Geoff Teece, Franklin Watts 2003

Keystones: Sikh Gurdwara
Kanwaljit Kaur Singh, A & C Black 2000

Websites
www.allaboutsikhs.com
A very detailed site about Sikhism, with information about Sikh history, beliefs, customs and worship.

www.sikhnet.com
General information and news about Sikhism and events in the Sikh world.

www.sikhs.org
More information about Sikhism.

www.worldprayers.org
A collection of prayers from many different faiths and traditions.

Index